Taking God Out of the Equation

By
Mrs Augustina Emobolu Godsent

Taking God Out of the Equation

Author: Mrs Augustina Emobolu Godsent

Copyright © 2024 Mrs Augustina Emobolu Godsent

The right of Mrs Augustina Emobolu Godsent to be identified as author of this work has been asserted by the author in accordance with section 77 and 78 of the Copyright, Designs and Patents Act 1988.

ISBN 978-1-83538-483-1 (Paperback)
       978-1-83538-484-8 (E-Book)

Cover Design and Book Layout by:
   White Magic Studios
   www.whitemagicstudios.co.uk

Published by:
   Maple Publishers
   Fairbourne Drive, Atterbury,
   Milton Keynes,
   MK10 9RG, UK
   www.maplepublishers.com

A CIP catalogue record for this title is available from the British Library.

All rights reserved. No part of this book may be reproduced or translated by any form or by any means, electronic or mechanical, including photocopying, recording or by any information storage and retrieval system without written permission from the author.

The views expressed in this work are solely those of the author and do not necessarily reflect the views of the publisher, and the publisher hereby disclaims any responsibility for them.

CONTENTS

DEDICATION 4

ACKNOWLEDGMENT 5

FOREWORD 6

Chapter 1 – THE JOURNEY 8

Chapter 2 – THE VOICE DIRECTIONS 13

Chapter 3 – ADULTHOOD JOURNEY 16

ABOUT THE AUTHOR 22

DEDICATION

I dedicate this book to the Almighty God, the source of all life, strength, and wisdom. I thank Him for all the mercies I have enjoyed on my journey so far, and for more to come.

It is by His inspiration and grace this book was started and completed.

To all the young people that will read this book. My prayer is that it would inspire you to believe in the Word of God and in yourself. That you would come to a place where you know for sure that there is nothing impossible for God to achieve through you.

ACKNOWLEDGMENT

I want to say a big thank you to my lovely husband for the support and encouragement to achieved this.

Thank you, Pastor Olaolu Adesina, for all your prayers and push. You always said that it is doable.

To Doctor Mrs Mary Otuyele, a mother indeed that stood by me right from my days of youth, thank you.

Pastor Akinola Elegbe, thanks for the early days.

And to the best Mother in-law and Father in-law, Pastor Festus Ilesanmi-Azaka Pastor Mrs Helen Ilesanmi-Azaka. Every day is a blessing with you.

Thank you all!

FOREWORD

Day one! A child is born. Her cries fill the air round about her; but everyone is happy, laughing and congratulating her parents. Right from that instant, her journey begins in the new, big world.

Wait: what about the moments before that time? See, a person's journey begins long before that first cry. Two passages in the bible come to mind. First, *Genesis 25:23; "And the Lord said unto her, two nations are in thy womb, and two manner of people shall be separated from thy bowels; and the one people shall be stronger than the other people; and the elder shall serve the younger."*

Second, *Jeremiah 1:5; "Before I formed you in the womb I knew you, before you were born, I set you apart; I appointed you as a prophet to the nations."*

One can choose to either go through life engaging it in a game of trial and error, or one can go through life walking assuredly, knowing what they have been created to achieve, guided on how to achieve it, and guarded against the opposition that will rise because of being on this path.

The story in this book, told from a first-person perspective, shows the reader the practical effects of listening and either obeying or disobeying the voice of God.

If you want to standout, make it in life with as little hassle as possible, and fulfil the destiny God created you for, I encourage you to take the lessons from this book and adapt it to your life.

Day X: Silence! The end to which all must come. There are tears and sighs from all around.

Question: Was destiny fulfilled?

Chapter 1

THE JOURNEY

"*For I know the thoughts that I think toward you, says the Lord, thoughts of peace and not of evil, to give you a future and a hope." Jeremiah 29.11 NKJV.*

Taking God out of the equation of one's life usually ends with disaster. Such becomes a life without divine fulfilment, according to the word of God in Joshua 1:8.

Having a life with Jesus Christ as the foundation keeps you going and there is always an inner peace of mind regardless of the challenges of life, and this helps you to push further.

Losing dad at a tender age took quite a lot from me and my siblings. His sudden death caught everyone unawares, and there was no one who could have a conversation with us to understand how to deal with life after his passing. This forced me to reason as an adult from age 12 and there was so much to deal with. My dad was a very caring person; he would tell us things, take care of us, get school outfits, and show us his children, love that revealed how much he cherished us. But he was not perfect either. He made mistakes and did wrong things that hurt my mother, but he never disrespected her for once in our presence.

I was born into a Catholic family of nine children, and I was the last child. My family loved me so much and they spoilt me; I had everything I needed to wear and spend whenever I needed them, and no one ever said no to me. Although my family was not rich, we were comfortable.

I am blessed in a way that the voice of God has always been audible to me right from a young age, but I did not understand what it was and no one around me was spiritually sound to explain it to me. Growing up in the Catholic Church did not help either in understanding the things of the spirit, because it takes spiritual discernment to have what it takes to know the voice of God.

Even at that, every step I took growing up, there was always a still voice that told me what to get involved with and what to avoid, and obeying, when instructed, always lead to a good ending for me. Many tagged me as very secretive; 'you cannot know her mind' and many other words were used to describe my personality. I differed from my schoolmates in the way I did things. Choosing friends as well, there was a leading inside of me that made me choose wisely those I got close to.

I did not understand it then, but I noticed that the decisions I made were always right and my parents confirmed it too. They would say most times, "Whatever she wants to do kindly allow her to do it", but my siblings believed it was because I was the last child of the family.

The journey continued with the help of the Holy Spirit and good friends. I finished my secondary school with good grades and looked for admission to university. Sitting for exams to enter university, I spent 4 good years at home waiting to pass the Joint Admissions and Matriculation Board (JAMB) exam. I was advised to get an application form from the University of Ilorin, Kwara State, Nigeria and then use that as a point of entry to the main university to study economics. And I did. But when I went to the university to pay for the admission form, I discovered my name was not in the list of the students that were selected.

A friend brought up a new opportunity to get an admission form from a different university. There was a mutual friend who knew someone that would help me get the form to enter through the Diploma course and then get in after the first year into the university degree to study Economics. Luckily for me, my name was among the selected students. So, I was thrilled when saw it, and then went home to tell my mum about it. She gave me the school fees, and I secured accommodation in an excellent area.

This friend who brought the opportunity to my attention asked me to wait for her to secure the school fees from her parents so the both of us would make the payment together; my spirit told me not to do that, but I allowed my emotions to take the upper-hand and I did not listen to the still voice. Time passed, and I waited for this friend, but in the end, I was disappointed. I only found out later from a mutual friend that she went to the university without my knowledge to pay the fees.

Surprise and fear came over me. I did not want my mum to know that I was yet to pay the fees she gave me a long time ago. So, I travelled down to the university to pay the school fees, but they rejected it because it was already past the closing date. Tears dropped from my eyes because I disobeyed the leading in my spirit. I went back home and told my mum, and we tried everything, but there was no way to get in anymore. This was what made me to attend a polytechnic instead of a university and it was part-time studies because there was no available space for full-time admission.

In polytechnic, I started making new friends and trying to be a big girl by having relationships.

There were so many distractions, but still the voice of God and His hands were very much alive in my life. Sometimes the voice would tell me when to avoid going to school because there would be a big and violent fight amongst the bad guys (cultists) which would cause the government of the state to close the school.

So much time was wasted in that period, but I completed my studies successfully. Then the next stage of my life started with the opportunity to travel aboard.

Chapter 2

THE VOICE DIRECTIONS

When grandmother was to be buried, we all went to the village for the ceremony and the planning was big. All the children and the grandchildren (from my mum and the other siblings) were around, too. On the big day I heard the voice say to me: "Do not wear the party clothes like everyone else", so, I had put on a pair of jeans and T-shirt instead. I informed my mum about it and she said that it was fine and to follow the leading of the voice. One of my siblings was unhappy about it and asked me to be the errand girl for the day. When guests came to shower money on my mum as she danced and some fell on the floor, she made me gather them up so that many people will not realise I was part of the family and instead see me as a house help to the family; not knowing that God was protecting me from the upcoming disaster. Everyone who wore the party clothes, including the guests, had issues I cannot detail for confidentiality reasons.

In another experience I had of the voice leadings, one of my siblings who was living in another state at the time needed something and I offered to take it there. When the day of travel came, I went with a male friend of mine on the journey. We delivered the message safely and on our way back; the voice told me not to enter a particular bus for the journey back to my state. I explained to my friend that this was what my spirit was saying because it was late and it was getting dark.

He dismissed what I said and pointed out that the bus needed only two passengers to start the journey. He asked me to forget what my mind was saying, and once again I allowed emotions to take the upper-hand and we went on the bus. On the bus, I made a prayer without understanding the danger of what I prayed for. "Oh Lord, if anything should happen for not following this still voice, please take my life in replacement of everyone inside the bus". It was a naïve prayer because not long after that, there was a problem with the bus and we were involved in a serious accident. The bus somersaulted over three times completely right off the road, but thankfully everyone came out alive. But my handbag went missing. The still voice said to me it was a replacement for my life. My friend was scared to death, and he apologised for not listening to me earlier when I told him what I had heard.

Several times, the voice guided me on what to keep to myself, where to go and where not to go. Many things happened by following the still voice, secrets revealed to me, both physically and spiritually. Despite my background of a lack of spiritual understanding, God was still faithfully guiding me every step of my life.

Pay attention to your dreams, the still voice in your soul that tells you the right things to do and warns you from destruction; studying the word of God is another way to hear from Him. Use the word with your mouth and declare it to your environment. Then things will definitely work for you. Obedience is the major key required to stay connected, and it allows the plan of God to come to full manifestation.

Chapter 3

ADULTHOOD JOURNEY

Although the parents or adults involved in your upbringing can determine how far you go in achieving destiny; not having a parent or anyone to train you is not an excuse to fail in life. Be mindful of the people who you surround yourself with as you grow and learn because their presence in your life will most likely influence if/how far you will achieve your goals and fulfil destiny.

Many things happened to me in my twenties, but I will share some relevant ones that will help any young person reading this book. The moment you take God out of the equation of your life is the moment you set yourself up for errors, heartbreaks, betrayals, sins, bad friends, and bad influence. Please pay good attention to this, especially if as a young person you want to go far in life and fulfil destiny. God is always important on the journey of your life; involving Him will help you know the purpose of why you were created and avoid delays on the journey of life.

There were many sources of distraction in my twenties-for example, during the period I spent studying in the polytechnic in Nigeria, I attracted lots of attention because everything I wanted my mum gave me. I had one of my siblings' cars to drive to school. Friends, some very good friends, and some that are friends with you for what they can gain from you constantly surrounded me. One day I started thinking about my life: I wondered where my life was headed, and what plans I had to achieve my goals. Looking at the people who were around me, friends, and family, I knew it was not possible to go far in life with the lifestyle and the environment I was growing up in. The overwhelming majority were young people eager to make money, both male and female. In the same environment, we heard of people that were very intelligent. We also heard of the ones that were getting pregnant; and there were those who were smoking dangerous substances and so on.

There was really no role model to follow except one of my elder brothers, who taught me how to read and write. He left the country to study abroad and left me with his close friend to monitor my growth, and ensure that I kept the standard of decency that he required of me. This friend, Fred Elegbe, was my private English tutor and a wonderful mentor who bought me my first bible to study. When I had the opportunity to study abroad, he helped me with my applications, and followed me to the interview. He was indeed a God-sent to me. Now a pastor, he is devoted to helping young people to fulfil their destiny, which does not surprise me because he has always been very passionate about the younger generation.

I was granted a visa to study abroad, and my entire world changed. The long journey to the United Kingdom started with the flight booked-it was 12 hours on the plane! While on the flight, I couldn't sleep. I kept on mediating on the things around the plane: the height, people inside the plane, etc. Few hours to land, I could not help but admire the amazing view that was before me. So, I said in my mind, 'God, I want to know you because with all these things I can see, there is no way anyone can say God does not exist.' We landed in Heathrow Airport. I went through the check and got my bags and as I was walking towards the exit door, I heard a voice say to me: my daughter, if you don't serve me you will die young. The voice said confess me as your Lord and saviour and at that spot He asked me to go on my knees, and told me to repent.

I repeated the words as I heard them: 'I accept you Lord as my Lord and Saviour, and I surrender my life to you. Amen.' That was how I gave my life to Christ Jesus, a personal encounter which was a great experience and one of the best things that ever happened to me. My life changed completely, and it was at that point I understood that the voice speaking to me right from my young age was the voice of God. I began studying the word of God. A significant benefit for me was I joined my elder brother, who was a born-again Christian here in the United Kingdom. He was always available to explain anything in the bible that was not clear to me. The journey of my spiritual growth started in Christ.

I also started attending classes and libraries, which was the primary reason I came to the United Kingdom. It was very hard. The school fees were real struggles. Being a young believer in my twenties, I was very naïve and thought the body of Christ was there to help you financially, spiritually, emotionally, and so on. This was when the struggle started. My life turned around in such a way that I learnt to depend on God before making decisions, and He always came through for me. Many things happened to me that took me away from the plan of God before mercy found me and God gave me a second chance on the journey of life. Ups and downs, wrong decisions, mingled with wrong people that discouraged me with words like: 'you cannot do this and that because you are a black person in such an environment' which was a lie. God picked my life from there and turned it around for the better.

One of the major setbacks for me was the betrayal of the people that called themselves believers, the people that claim to be righteous, people that preach the word of God without following what they preached. Looking unto people for help, both family and friends made me suffer so much. My university fees were a struggle, but eventually, God did it and I graduated.

The one thing that kept me going was the word of God. The promises in his word made me learn to keep going and never to give up. In Jeremiah 29 verses 12 to 14 it says, "Then you will call upon Me and go and pray to Me, and I will listen you. And you will seek Me and find Me, when you search for me with all your heart. I will be found by you, says the Lord, and I will bring you back from your captivity; I will gather you from all the nations and from all the places where I have driven you, says the Lord, and I will bring you to the place from which I cause you to be carried away captive."

Always have in mind that the thoughts of God for your life is of good and not evil, which will take you to an expected end as long as you do not give up on God. Never allow anything to stop you on the journey of life; either background, environment, friendship and so on. If God can change my life and make it useful to Him regardless of status, He is too faithful not to fulfil His plans for your life. Remember, anyone that takes out from the equation of their life the Lord Jesus Christ (the Word of God) ends up in destruction.

ABOUT THE AUTHOR

Mrs Augustina Emobolu Godsent is a gospel singer serving under Pastor Olaolu Adesina of MFM Southampton United Kingdom. She is passionate about helping others, especially the young people.

She holds a Bachelor of Arts (BA) Business Studies from the University of Gloucestershire United Kingdom, diploma in Accounting and Finance from the Marlborough College of Business and Technology United Kingdom.

She also received further training at the London School of Commerce seminar in their 2012 Management Development Programme.

She is married to Ohilebo Godsent Ilesanmi-Azaka, and they are blessed with two children. Theirs is a family devoted to the things of God; making sure that the gospel of our Lord Jesus Christ reaches to all the world through word and music.

www.ingramcontent.com/pod-product-compliance
Lightning Source LLC
Chambersburg PA
CBHW070344120526
44590CB00017B/3003